Canada
For Kids
People, Places and Cultures
Children Explore The World Books

SPEEDY
PUBLISHING

Speedy Publishing LLC
40 E. Main St. #1156
Newark, DE 19711
www.speedypublishing.com

Let's learn some interesting facts about Canada!

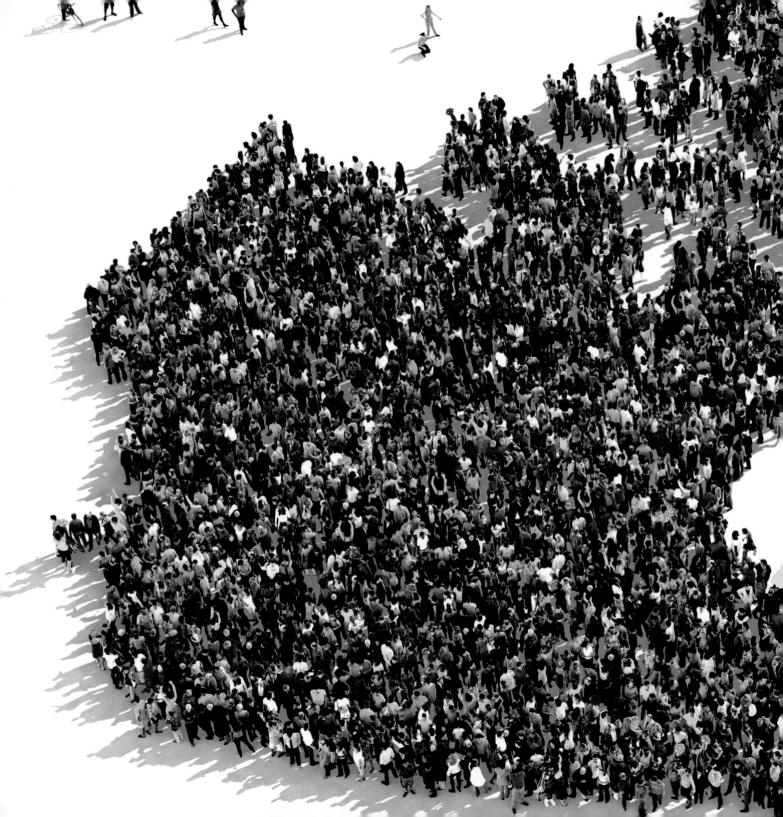

In 2012 the population of Canada was around 35 million.

The 2 main languages spoken in Canada are English and French.

Canada is the
second largest
country in
the world by
total area .

The maple leaf is a Canadian symbol and features prominently on the national flag.

The Canadian motto, A Mari Usque ad Mare, means "From sea to sea."

Canada features the longest coastline in the world, stretching 202080 kilometres (125570 miles).

Canada shares the longest land border in the world with the United States, totaling 8891 kilometres (5525 miles).

Canada is also home to the longest street in the world. Yonge Street in Ontario starts at Lake Ontario, and runs north through Ontario to the Minnesota border, a distance of almost 2000 kilometres.

Canada has
over 30000
lakes.

Winters can be very cold in Canada with temperatures dropping below -40 °C (-40 °F) in some parts of the country.

Canada's longest river is the McKenzie River in the North West. The river is 2,635miles or 4,241km long.

The highest
mountain in
Canada is
with 19,551ft
or 5,959m the
Mount Logan
in the Yukon
Territory at
the border
with Alaska.

Canada has the largest waterfalls by water volume. These are the Niagara Falls.

Canada is home to about 55,000 different species of insects.

Canada is the second largest oil reserve holder after Saudi Arabia.

Most of the Canadian families have roots in England and France, as during the French and British colonised the country and thus many families from 'the old world' immigrated into Canada.

Inuit are Canada's indigenous people

Canada has a lot to offer and you should visit the country soon and explore!

Published by
Speedy Publishing LLC
40 E. Main St., #1156
Newark DE 19711

Cover by 24HR Covers